First Biographies
Tomie dePaola

by Eric Braun

Consulting Editor: Gail Saunders-Smith, PhD

Capstone
press

Mankato, Minnesota

Pebble Books are published by Capstone Press,
151 Good Counsel Drive, P.O. Box 669, Mankato, Minnesota 56002.
www.capstonepress.com

1 2 3 4 5 6 10 09 08 07 06 05

Library of Congress Cataloging-in-Publication Data
Braun, Eric, 1971–
    Tomie dePaola / by Eric Braun.
    p. cm.—(First biographies)
    ISBN-13: 978-0-7368-3641-8 (hardcover)
    ISBN-10: 0-7368-3641-1 (hardcover)
    ISBN-13: 978-0-7368-5093-3 (softcover pbk.)
    ISBN-10: 0-7368-5093-7 (softcover pbk.)
    1. De Paola, Tomie—Juvenile literature. 2. Authors, American—20th century—
Biography—Juvenile literature. 3. Illustrators—United States—Biography—Juvenile
literature. 4. Children's stories—Authorship—Juvenile literature. I. Title. II. First
biographies (Mankato, Minn.)
PS3554.E1147Z58 2005
813'.54—dc22   2004013483

Summary: Simple text and photographs present the life of Tomie dePaola.

Note to Parents and Teachers

The First Biographies set supports national history standards for units on
people and culture. This book describes and illustrates the life of Tomie
dePaola. The images support early readers in understanding the text. The
repetition of words and phrases helps early readers learn new words. This
book also introduces early readers to subject-specific vocabulary words,
which are defined in the Glossary section. Early readers may need
assistance to read some words and to use the Table of Contents, Glossary,
Read More, Internet Sites, and Index sections of the book.

Table of Contents

Time Line

1934
born

Early Years

Tomie dePaola was born in Connecticut in 1934. Tomie's mother read to him. When Tomie was 4, he knew he wanted to write and draw.

Tomie's hometown, Meriden, Connecticut, in 1934

Time Line

1934
born

1952
goes to
art school

Tomie drew lots of pictures as he grew up. He graduated from high school in 1952. He went to art school in New York.

Pratt Art Institute in New York, where Tomie went to art school

Time Line

Tomie went to the
Museum of Modern Art
whenever he could.
He looked at the paintings
to learn more about art.

◀ Museum of Modern Art, New York. Visitors look at
art by Ben Shahn, a famous artist whom Tomie liked.

Time Line

1934
born

1952
goes to
art school

1962
becomes an
art teacher

First Jobs

Tomie became an
art teacher after college.
In 1965, he drew pictures
for a science book.
It was his first job
as a book illustrator.

Newton College in Massachusetts, where Tomie
worked as an art teacher

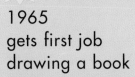

1965
gets first job
drawing a book

Time Line

1934
born

1952
goes to
art school

1962
becomes an
art teacher

Tomie's Books

The first book Tomie wrote and illustrated was *The Wonderful Dragon of Timlin.* He made more books in the next few years.

◀ Tomie painting a picture in his studio

1965
gets first job
drawing a book

1966
first book is
published

Time Line

```
     1934              1952              1962
     born              goes to           becomes an
                       art school        art teacher
```

Tomie made a book
called *Nana Upstairs &
Nana Downstairs*. Children
enjoy this book about
Tomie's grandmothers.

1965
gets first job
drawing a book

1966
first book is
published

Time Line

1934
born

1952
goes to
art school

1962
becomes an
art teacher

Tomie kept teaching art.
He kept writing
and illustrating books.
Kids love his books.
Adults do, too.

1965
gets first job
drawing a book

1966
first book is
published

Time Line

1934
born

1952
goes to
art school

1962
becomes an
art teacher

Tomie makes fun books.
Bonjour, Mr. Satie is
about a traveling cat.
Strega Nona is about
an old woman and
a magic pot.

◀ Tomie with a large picture from *Bonjour, Mr. Satie*

1965
gets first job
drawing a book

1966
first book is
published

1991
Bonjour, Mr. Satie
is published

Time Line

1934
born

1952
goes to
art school

1962
becomes an
art teacher

Tomie has illustrated
more than 200 books.
He has won many awards.
Tomie plans to
keep making books
for a long time.

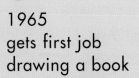

1965
gets first job
drawing a book

1966
first book is
published

1991
Bonjour, Mr. Satie
is published

21

Glossary

art—something beautiful that is made by drawing, painting, or crafting by hand

college—a school students go to after high school

graduate—to finish all required classes at a school

illustrate—to draw pictures for a book or other publication; people who draw pictures for books are called illustrators.

Read More

dePaola, Tomie. *Four Friends in Autumn.* New York: Simon & Schuster Books for Young Readers, 2004.

dePaola, Tomie. *Stagestruck.* New York: G. P. Putnam's Sons, 2005.

Woods, Mae. *Tomie dePaola.* Children's Authors. Edina, Minn.: Abdo, 2000.

Internet Sites

FactHound offers a safe, fun way to find Internet sites related to this book. All of the sites on FactHound have been researched by our staff.

Here's how:

1. Visit *www.facthound.com*
2. Type in this special code **0736836411** for age-appropriate sites. Or enter a search word related to this book for a more general search.
3. Click on the **Fetch It** button.

FactHound will fetch the best sites for you!

Index

Word Count: 196
Grade: 1
Early-Intervention Level: 16

Editorial Credits
Mari C. Schuh, editor; Heather Kindseth, set designer; Patrick D. Dentinger,
 book designer; Kelly Garvin, photo researcher; Scott Thoms, photo editor

Photo Credits
Capstone Press/Karon Dubke, 14
Corbis/Schenectady Museum; Hall of Electrical History Foundation, 4
Courtesy of Pratt Institute, 6
Getty Images Inc./Hulton Archive, 8
Globe Photos/Adam Scull, 18
John J. Burns Library, Boston College, 10
2004 Suki Coughlin Photography/Paula McFarland Stylist, cover, 1, 12, 16, 20

I saw a PURPLE COW

and 100 Other Recipes for Learning

I saw a Purple Cow

and 100 Other Recipes for Learning

by
Ann Cole, Carolyn Haas,
Faith Bushnell and Betty Weinberger

Illustrated by True Kelley

LITTLE, BROWN AND COMPANY
Boston   Toronto

Fifth Printing

T11/72

Library of Congress Cataloging in Publication Data
Main entry under title:

I saw a purple cow.

   1. Education, Preschool. 2. Domestic education.
I. Cole, Ann.
LB1140.2.I2   372.1'3   72-404
ISBN 0-316-15174-2
ISBN 0-316-15175-0 (pbk)

*Published simultaneously in Canada
by Little, Brown & Company (Canada) Limited*

PRINTED IN THE UNITED STATES OF AMERICA

To our children
Gary, Laura, Danny and Nancy Cole
Andy, Mari, Betsy, Tom and Karen Haas
George III, Christie, Elizabeth and Stuart Bushnell
John and Beth Weinberger

and to our husbands
Roger, Bob, George and Stanley

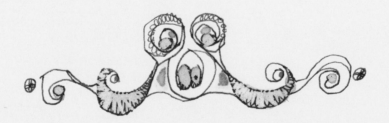

ACKNOWLEDGMENTS

Can too many cooks spoil the broth? Sometimes . . . In our case, however, we feel that four authors, plus a variety of experts, have enriched the potpourri. All along the way, we sought the advice of specialists in the field of early childhood: teachers, curriculum consultants, parent coordinators, social workers, psychiatrists, recreational therapists, pediatricians, as well as editors and publishers of children's literature. Each individual added his own particular dimension and emphasis to the growth and direction of our total project.

We are especially grateful to the parents from the St. Cecilia and Horizon House Headstart Centers in Chicago, who tested our ideas and shared many of their own; and to Lillian Tauber, Sara Lemon, Ruth Ellis, Mary Knaus, Virginia Coleman, Frances Murray and William Okrafasmart, who "opened the door" for this Headstart pilot study.

We are indebted to Carol Heidemann, Barbara Bowman, Joanne Wiley, Dorcas Bowles and Bernard Berkin, whose critical judgment and evaluation helped us to clarify our goals. We appreciate the guidance and support that Arnita Boswell, Harold Richman, Jay Hirsch, Gerald Fleishner, Catherine Hudson, Perle Abrahamson, Mary Woolfington and the late Sadie Nesbitt have given us from the beginning.

Our thanks also go to Elizabeth Heller, Holly Kempner and Connie James, whose artwork enhanced our presentation; and to Susan Terris, who found Bonnie Bryant, who brought our manuscript to editors Ralph Woodward and John Keller of Little, Brown. Finally, each of us wishes to thank the other three for their patience, perseverance and friendship.

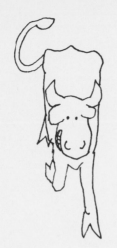

INTRODUCTION

"I saw a purple cow" . . . I "one" him, I "two" him, I "three" him . . . I *"eight"* him! A whimsical game, written simply, yet offering much: an approach to learning through play with numbers, words and colors, a key to unlock a child's imagination, a time for laughter and communicating with others, one of many shared experiences which can influence a child's future attitude toward learning.

Although every moment of a child's life is learning time, no period is as important as the six preschool years. The parent, as the child's first teacher, plays the key role in these critical years. Yet, unlike the child's later teachers, the parent faces this challenge with no formal training and few practical guidelines.

I Saw a Purple Cow and 100 Other Recipes for Learning grew out of the authors' desire to support parents in their role as early educators by offering them concrete and creative learning activities in an easy-to-use format. To this end, we embarked on a four-year project, gathering ideas, turning our kitchens into "learning laboratories" with our children, and finally testing the activities through workshops for parents and staff in over thirty Headstart, day care and other preschool centers.

The result of our combined efforts is this collection of "learning recipes" — a preschool curriculum for the home. It includes the subjects of creating, pretending, exploring, music and rhythm, parties and learning games. Many of the activities were specifically selected to emphasize what a child can learn through his everyday experiences. For example, a trip to the grocery store can teach him to observe colors, sizes, textures and shapes; a simple "Rainy Day Walk in the House" can contribute as much to a young child's discovery as a distant field trip. A homemade puppet show, using some old socks, cardboard tubes, and a blanket thrown over a chair or table, can become an afternoon's project for the whole neighborhood. Music activities, beginning with simple finger games, can progress to a complete rhythm band of shoe box banjos, cardboard maracas, and humming flutes!

The activities found in this book are fun and easy to do. Most require only a few "throwaway" household items that, instead, can be saved and recycled for learning. Some require no materials at all. The step-by-step recipe format makes it easy to get a project or game under way quickly. However, these recipes are merely suggestions. Each child will approach an activity in his own way, and we hope he will find that the joy is in the doing as much as in the finished product. These suggestions can be enjoyed by a child alone or with his older brothers and sisters; on "sick-in-bed" days or while on a long car ride. There is a recipe for almost every situation. Symbols in the table of contents make it possible to find the appropriate activity quickly, including those which help to develop math and reading readiness.

The flexible nature of the activities allows a Headstart worker or a hospital volunteer, a student teacher or even a teenage babysitter to adapt these ideas to his particular needs. With the increase in the number of working mothers, and the resulting need for quality day care, *I Saw a Purple Cow and 100 Other Recipes for Learning* can provide an effective teaching tool for those involved in both public and private day care in homes and centers.

Our hope is that these hundred recipes will guide parents and professionals in helping children learn, observe, explore, discover, imagine, and who knows, maybe even see a purple cow!

CONTENTS

Many of the activities in this book are particularly useful to parents, teachers and children in specific situations or with particular educational goals. The symbols mean:

[S] Sick in bed   [M] Math readiness

[car] Traveling or waiting   [R] Reading readiness

USEFUL TO SAVE

Most everything you need can be found around the house.
Buy only the essentials and save the following:

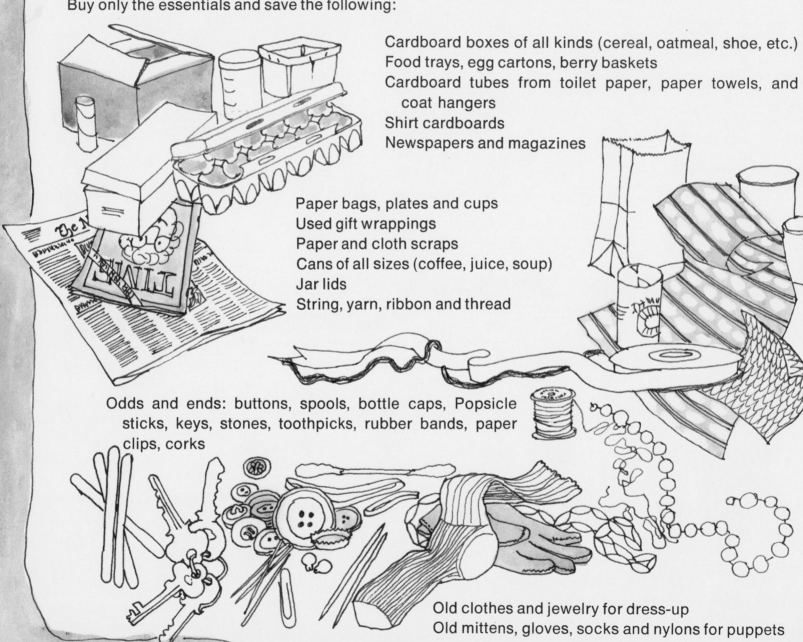

Cardboard boxes of all kinds (cereal, oatmeal, shoe, etc.)
Food trays, egg cartons, berry baskets
Cardboard tubes from toilet paper, paper towels, and
    coat hangers
Shirt cardboards
Newspapers and magazines

Paper bags, plates and cups
Used gift wrappings
Paper and cloth scraps
Cans of all sizes (coffee, juice, soup)
Jar lids
String, yarn, ribbon and thread

Odds and ends: buttons, spools, bottle caps, Popsicle
sticks, keys, stones, toothpicks, rubber bands, paper
clips, corks

Old clothes and jewelry for dress-up
Old mittens, gloves, socks and nylons for puppets

USEFUL TO BUY

The following items will provide the necessities for your supply kit:

Crayons, pencils, felt markers

Scissors

Construction paper, crepe and tissue paper
Watercolors or tempera paint

White glue, masking tape, cellophane tape

BASIC RECIPES

Paste

YOU NEED: 1 cup flour
½ cup water

YOU DO: 1) Combine the flour and water and mix until creamy.
2) Store in a covered container.
(For a more durable paste, add ½ cup flour to 1 cup *boiling* water. Stir over low heat until thick and shiny.)

Paste is excellent when working with paper (for example, torn paper collages). Glue is useful when a more lasting effect is desired, such as with macaroni or dried bean decorations.

Finger Paint

YOU NEED: paste mixed with an equal amount of liquid detergent
or
laundry starch (liquid)
food coloring or paint

YOU DO: 1) Add coloring to your paste mixture or laundry starch.
2) Dampen a piece of paper (shelf or butcher works the best) and drop on several teaspoons of finger paint. You can use one or more colors.
3) Swirl the paint around and around, changing the design as many times as you wish.

4) Spread your completed paintings out on newspaper to dry, or hang them up on a clothesline.

Finger-painting can be messy. Be sure to roll up your sleeves and wear an old shirt or a smock. Put newspaper under your paper or work directly on a plastic-topped table. (You can "pull a print" by laying a piece of paper *over* the painted surface and then peeling it off.)

Fun Dough

YOU NEED:
1½ cups flour
½ cup salt
½ cup water
¼ cup vegetable oil *or* a few drops of liquid detergent
food coloring (optional)

YOU DO:
1) Mix the flour and salt together in a bowl.
2) Slowly add the water, oil (or detergent) and food coloring.
3) Knead the dough well and shape into several balls. *Makes enough for two people.*

Now you have your own clay-dough! You can roll it, poke it, make it into animals, "cookies," "cakes," balls, holiday ornaments, or other objects.

For added fun, use sticks, cookie cutters, pencils, spoons, hair rollers, bottle caps or round blocks for rolling and cutting the dough.

Put the remaining dough in a tightly closed container or plastic bag and keep in the refrigerator, to be used again another day. If it becomes too sticky, add more flour.

Cornstarch Clay

YOU NEED: 1 cup cornstarch
2 cups salt
1⅓ cups cold water

YOU DO:

1) Put salt and ⅔ cup water in a pot and bring to a boil.
2) Mix cornstarch with remaining water and stir well.
3) Blend these 2 mixtures together and knead into clay. *Makes 3 cups.*
4) Mold the clay into various shapes or objects and let dry (takes several hours).
5) Paint them when they are dry, if you wish.
6) Unused clay must be kept in a covered jar or plastic bag in the refrigerator, to be used another day.

Cornstarch clay is a smooth-textured, pliable material for making objects you may wish to keep or give as gifts (candle holders, ashtrays, figures, wall plaques, etc.).

HOLIDAY ORNAMENTS

To make holiday ornaments from Cornstarch Clay or Fun Dough:

1) Roll out the clay or dough; then cut out bells, gingerbread men, etc.
2) Poke a hole near the top of your figure with a straw or pencil.
3) Bake the Fun Dough at 225° for 2 hours, turning figures 3 or 4 times to prevent curling.
4) Color with tempera paints and glue on glitter or sequins.
5) Use ornament hooks, string or yarn for hanging.

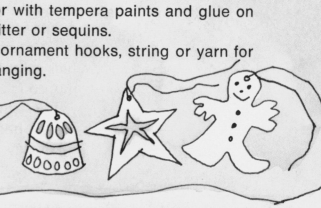

Make Believe

It's always fun to make believe you're someone else.

BE A DOCTOR OR A NURSE:
Make a stethoscope with a spool wrapped in foil and tied onto a string. Use clean rags for slings and bandages.

A POLICEMAN OR FIREMAN:
Wear a badge made of foil over cardboard (tape a safety pin to the back).

A FAIRY PRINCESS:
Dress up in a crown made of colored paper or foil. Use a stick for a wand; wrap it with foil and glue a star on top.

A PIRATE:
Tie a bandana on your head, put a patch over your eye. Make pirate earrings to hang over your ears: just loop a thread through an old button and tie the ends together.

AN INDIAN BRAVE:
Cut out feathers from construction paper or from the Sunday comics, and paste them on a paper headband. (Use cardboard, Popsicle sticks or straws behind *each* feather to make them stand up.) Make a tom-tom from a coffee can, and a tomahawk with construction paper and a stick.

You can be in the next room and yet think that you are far, far away.

MAKE A FARAWAY HIDEOUT:

1) Throw an old sheet, blanket or spread over a small table or two chairs.
2) Crawl inside with a few favorite toys and a flashlight. Pretend it's a fort or a house, a fire station or pirate ship, a cave or a castle, or whatever you want it to be.

TAKE A PRETEND TRIP:

1) A simple box or shopping bag can become a suitcase. Pack your clothes and get ready to go.
2) Cut out magazine pictures of places you want to visit.
3) Make your own tickets out of paper.
4) Line up some chairs for a train or bus . . . and off you go!

OPEN YOUR OWN GROCERY STORE:

1) Use a table or some large boxes for counters and shelves.
2) Stock your store with empty cans, boxes, jars, egg cartons, etc.
3) Mark the prices, make some play money, and don't forget a cash box.
4) Now invite your friends to come and shop.

Grown-up Clothes

Ask Mom and Dad if they have any old clothes that you can use for "dress-up." Keep them in a *special* box or drawer for a rainy day.

Old hats, scarves and gloves
Pocketbooks filled with odds and ends
Ties, belts and vests
High-heeled shoes and boots
Long skirts, half-slips, shawls and veils

Sparkly jewelry—dangling earrings, beads and bracelets
Compacts and empty lipsticks
Eyeglass frames
Broken watches

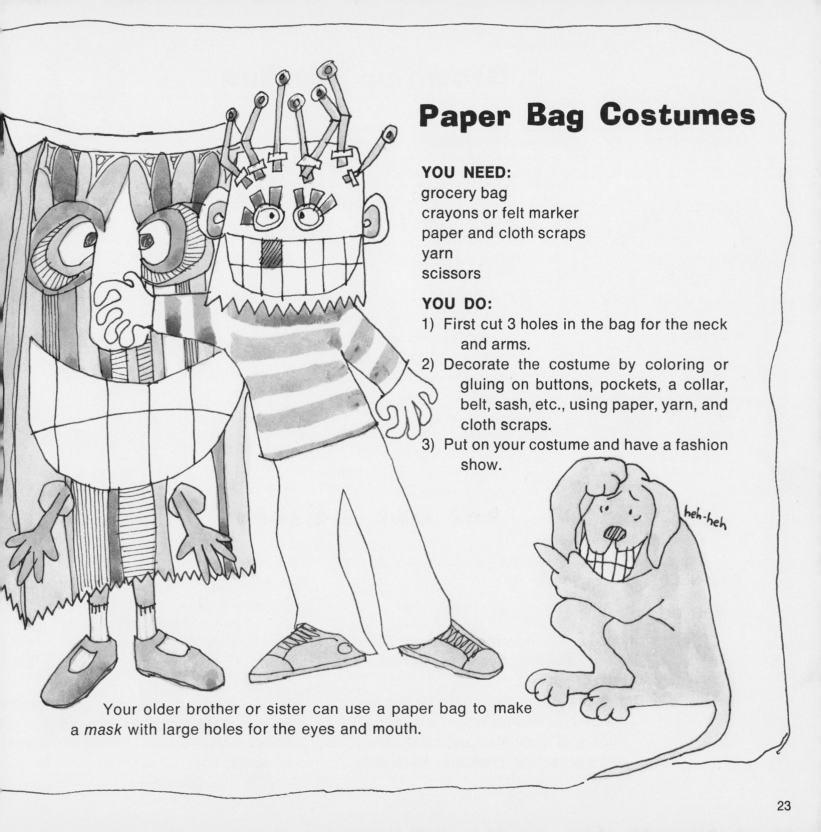

Paper Bag Costumes

YOU NEED:
grocery bag
crayons or felt marker
paper and cloth scraps
yarn
scissors

YOU DO:
1) First cut 3 holes in the bag for the neck and arms.
2) Decorate the costume by coloring or gluing on buttons, pockets, a collar, belt, sash, etc., using paper, yarn, and cloth scraps.
3) Put on your costume and have a fashion show.

heh-heh

Your older brother or sister can use a paper bag to make a *mask* with large holes for the eyes and mouth.

Papa Bear
Said.....

Act Out a Story

YOU NEED: a storybook

YOU DO:

1) Choose a favorite story (like *Peter Rabbit* or *The Three Bears*) for Mother to read or tell.
2) During the story pretend to do whatever the storybook characters are doing. If there is more than one child, each can choose the character he wants to be.

3) Use whatever is at hand for props and scenery:
   a rug can be a lake
   a chair can be a car
   or use no props at all, just your imagination!
4) With a very young child, the storyteller can stop at a familiar word and let the child fill it in. "Someone's been eating my _____."
   (porridge)

Bubbles in the Sink

YOU NEED: an apron or a towel around you to keep
your clothes dry
a little water in a sink or bowl
detergent or soap flakes
egg beater, sponges, funnel, baster, spoon,
jar lid, or anything unbreakable
measuring cups, milk cartons

YOU DO:
1) Roll up your sleeves.
2) Beat up mounds of suds and dump in
all your "kitchen toys." Try measuring and pouring water from one container to another.
3) Wipe up puddles when you are through.

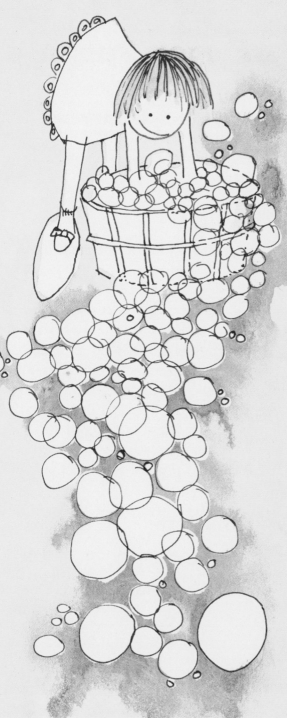

Monday's Washday

YOU NEED: doll clothes, hankies, and socks
pan or pail of suds
string clothesline
clothespins

YOU DO:
1) Put up your string clothesline between
2 chairs, bathroom hooks or kitchen
drawer handles.
2) Wash and rinse your clothes; squeeze
them well and use clothespins to
hang them up to dry.

Can you fold them in a pile?

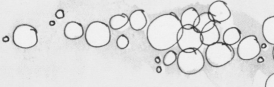

Finger Puppets

YOU NEED:
small ball (rubber, styrofoam, cork)
cotton or yarn
small buttons, sequins or cloth scraps
handkerchief
glue

YOU DO:
1) Poke a hole in the ball the size of your finger.
2) Make eyes, nose and mouth on the ball by gluing on buttons, sequins or bits of cloth.
3) Add yarn or cotton for hair.
4) Push a handkerchief or a square piece of fabric into the hole with your finger. Wiggle your finger and let your puppet "talk"! It might be fun to put a different face on each side of the ball, or to make several puppets for your fingers.

Paper Puppets

YOU NEED:
construction paper
scissors
crayons
glue
masking tape
Popsicle sticks or cardboard tubes

YOU DO:
1) Draw and cut out the outline of an animal or person from construction paper.
2) Draw or glue on eyes, nose and mouth, hair, hat, etc.
3) Tape a stick or tube to the back for support, leaving enough for a handle.

Tube and Clothespin Puppets

Use a toilet paper *tube* for the body and a Popsicle stick (taped inside) for the handle. Add face, arms, clothes, etc.

Decorate a wood *clothespin* with scraps of paper and cloth. Draw on a face and add yarn for the hair.

Sock Puppets

YOU NEED: old glove, mitten or sock
newspaper, rags or old stockings for stuffing
cardboard tube from coat hanger, stick or ruler
string or rubber band
paint and felt marker
paper and cloth scraps
yarn

YOU DO:
1) Stuff the sock, glove or mitten with newspaper, rags or an old stocking.
2) Push the stick, cardboard tube or ruler into the puppet (for a handle) and secure it with a string or rubber band.
3) Draw or paint on a face and use yarn for hair; dress it up with paper or cloth scraps.

Another easy way to make a puppet is to sew or glue eyes and hair on the sock or mitten, put it on your hand, and use your fingers and thumb to open and close the "mouth."

Talk to your puppet and let it "talk" to you.

27

Let's Put on a Puppet Show

YOU NEED: puppets you have made
large box, open on one side
table or chair
clothesline and sheet or blanket (optional)

YOU DO:
1) Cut out a large square from the side of the box opposite the open side.
2) Set the box on a table or chair and sit on the floor behind it. Or you can kneel behind a couch or chair, or string a clothesline across a doorway and hang a sheet or blanket over it.
   The show is on!

String-Ting-a-Ling

YOU NEED: 2 paper cups or empty juice cans (cans work best)
a long string (15 or 20 feet)

YOU DO:
1) Poke a hole in the end of each cup or can.
2) Pull the string through the cans (open ends facing out) and knot the string at each end.
3) Now you take one can, and your partner takes the other and goes as far as the string will stretch. (Keep it taut.) Take turns talking into the can and listening to your partner on the other end of the "line."

Be a Switchboard Operator

YOU NEED: cardboard box, any size
paints or crayons
string, yarn or covered wire
large nails with heads (roofing nails are best)
paper cup
earmuffs (optional)

YOU DO: 1) Paint or color one side of the box, if you wish.

2) Mark 3 rows of dots on the painted side with a pencil or crayon. Poke a hole through each dot with a nail.

3) Cut the string, yarn or wire into 1-foot lengths, one for each hole in the *top row*. Push one end through each hole and knot it on the back.

4) Tie nails onto the dangling ends of the strings.

5) Poke both ends of a yard of string through a hole in the bottom of the paper cup. Knot the ends and hang the cup around your neck.

6) Now play "operator" by speaking into the cup and plugging the nails into different holes. A pair of earmuffs will do nicely for a headphone.

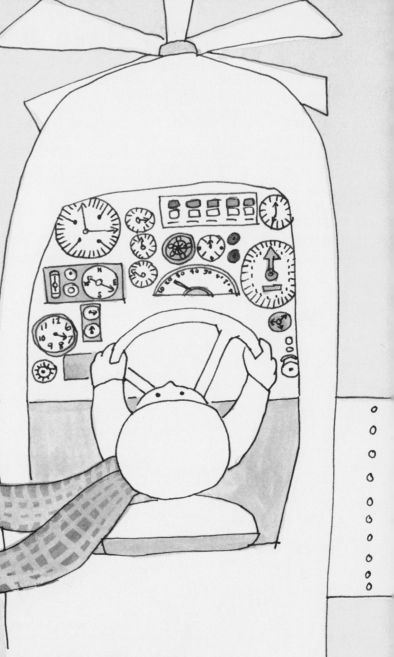

Instrument Panels

To make an instrument panel for an airplane, boat or car, glue a mirror, old spools and buttons onto a piece of cardboard or a cardboard box. Draw on the speedometer, clock, etc.

Let's Have a Cold Drink Stand

YOU NEED:

a small table or sturdy box

paper and crayons

pitcher

ice cubes

lemonade, fruitade or punch (fresh, frozen or packaged)

large spoon

paper or plastic cups

a few pennies, nickels and dimes to make change

money box

a bag for trash

YOU DO:

1) Set up a table or box in front of your house or on a nearby corner.
2) Make a sign with the paper and crayons.
3) Pour the drink into a pitcher and stir. (Ask for help with the directions on the package.)
4) Set out the cups and start selling.
5) Count your change carefully — and keep it in a safe place.
6) Clean everything up when you close for the day.

If you have a few helpers, you could add homemade cookies or candy to your stand. Now you're in business!

TODDLER TOYS

This section describes toys that a parent or older child might make for a toddler.

Stack-'Em-Up

YOU NEED: 3 or 4 empty cans of different sizes that will nest inside each other
nail polish or contact paper

YOU DO: 1) Remove the tops with a can opener and flatten the rough edges by pinching them with pliers. Ask your mother to help with this.

2) Soak off the labels. Wash and dry the cans.

3) Line them up in order of size.

4) Number the cans from smallest to largest, using nail polish, or cover the cans with contact paper. You might paste a different color on each can.

WHAT CAN YOU DO WITH YOUR SET OF CANS?

Stack them in a tower and knock them down again.

Ask your older brother or sister to hide a bottle cap or penny under one so you can guess where it is.

A three- or four-year-old might enjoy putting different-sized buttons or spools in each can with the smallest button in the smallest can, etc.

Nest the cans inside one another before putting them away.

Push-and-Pull Toys

YOU NEED:
round ice-cream, oatmeal or cornmeal carton
string
beans, pebbles or bottle caps
masking tape
construction paper, crepe paper or comic pages

Milk Carton Blocks

Save cardboard milk and juice cartons to make a set of toddler's blocks.
1) Cut off and tape down the tops, if they aren't flat.
2) Cartons covered with scraps of contact paper are both colorful and washable.

YOU DO:
1) Poke a hole in the center of the top and bottom of the box.
2) Knot one end of a long string and thread it through the hole on the *bottom* of the box.
3) Put a few beans, bottle caps or pebbles into the box to make it a rattle.
4) Pull the string through the *lid* and then tape the lid on.
5) Cover with brightly colored paper.

Leave off the string and you have a *rolling* toy.

My Own Mailbox

YOU NEED:
box with lid
crayons or tempera paint
scissors
letters, cards and small treasures

YOU DO:
1) Have a grown-up cut a slot in the lid of a cardboard box.
2) Color it to look like a mailbox.
3) Drop your letters, cards, and treasures through the slot, and dump them out again and again.

Shoe Box Trains

YOU NEED:
empty shoe boxes, cardboard vegetable
   trays, milk or egg cartons
scissors
construction paper or comic pages
crayons
buttons, tubes or spools
heavy string or cord

YOU DO:
1) Cover the boxes with comics or construction paper; decorate with crayons. You might want to color the last car red for the caboose.
2) You can draw or cut out windows on some of the boxes to look like passenger cars.
3) For wheels cut out and glue paper circles or buttons onto the sides of the boxes, or tape cardboard tubes or spools underneath.
4) Poke a small hole in the front and back ends of each box.
5) Tie a knot at one end of a long string and run it through all the boxes, allowing enough string at the front (engine) for pulling.

Now you can take your favorite dolls and stuffed animals for a ride.

SIMPLE CRAFTS

Loop Earrings

YOU NEED: round boxes (from cornmeal or oatmeal)
scissors
string or yarn
foil or crepe paper

YOU DO: 1) Let Mother "slice" the box into rings.
2) Wrap the rings with foil or crepe paper.
3) Loop a string or yarn through each ring and tie the ends together.

Now hang the earrings over your ears to be a gypsy, a queen or a pirate.

Cardboard disks and egg carton cups make pretty loop earrings, too.

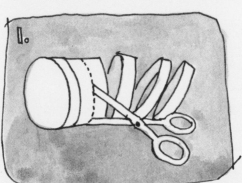

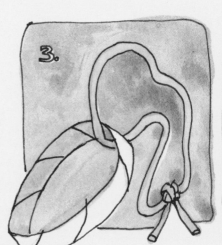

Macaroni Jewelry

YOU NEED: any kind of macaroni with a large hole
straws cut into small pieces
colored construction paper (optional)
string, yarn or shoelace
tape
food coloring (optional)

YOU DO:
1) For easy threading, make a tip on the yarn or string by wrapping a piece of tape tightly around one end.
2) String the macaroni or straws one at a time, being careful to tie on the first and last "bead."
3) Leave some string at each end for tying.
4) Short strings will make bracelets or earrings; longer ones, necklaces, belts and headbands.

FOR VARIETY:

Cut shapes out of construction paper, punch holes in the center with a pencil, and string them along with the macaroni or straws.

FOR ADDED COLOR:

Crayon or paint the macaroni or dye it the night before by dipping it into a small dish of food coloring mixed with water. Remove, using tongs, gloves or a spoon with holes; dry on waxed paper.

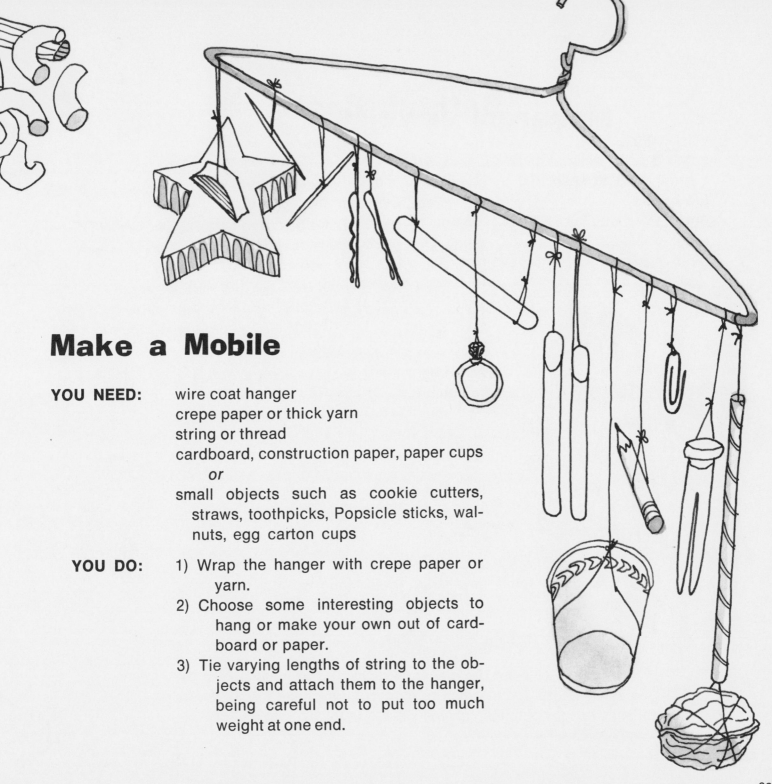

Make a Mobile

YOU NEED: wire coat hanger
crepe paper or thick yarn
string or thread
cardboard, construction paper, paper cups
  or
small objects such as cookie cutters, straws, toothpicks, Popsicle sticks, walnuts, egg carton cups

YOU DO: 1) Wrap the hanger with crepe paper or yarn.
2) Choose some interesting objects to hang or make your own out of cardboard or paper.
3) Tie varying lengths of string to the objects and attach them to the hanger, being careful not to put too much weight at one end.

Bathtub Boats

YOU NEED:
bottle cap or jar lid, bar of soap, cork or
   empty walnut shell
toothpicks
dab of Fun Dough or clay
crayons, scissors
cloth or paper

YOU DO:
1) Draw (and color) a sail; then cut it out.
   Put your name or a number on the
   sail if you wish.
2) Poke a toothpick through the sail.
3) Stick a dab of Fun Dough or clay inside the jar lid or shell (neither is
   needed for the cork or soap).
4) Now put the toothpick into the Fun
   Dough and your boat is ready to sail
   away!

Hint: When using a cork, push a penny into a slit in the
cork for balance.

Print a Pattern

YOU NEED: tempera paint (not too thin)
jar lids or muffin tin
potato, carrot, celery or sponge
small hard objects, such as keys, hair rollers or bottle caps
paper towels or newspaper
other paper, of any kind

YOU DO:
1) Spread newspaper over work area.
2) Cut a design into a potato or carrot (have Mother help with this).
3) Pour a small amount of paint into a jar lid or muffin tin.
4) Dip your vegetable or one of the other objects into the paint; blot first on paper towel or newspaper, then press it down on your paper.
5) Print a pattern by repeating the design over and over.

You can make wrapping paper, notepaper, greeting cards, or a picture.

COLLECTING

Patchwork Pictures

YOU NEED:
paper, box lid or food tray
glue
scraps of all kinds
scissors
Popsicle sticks and buttons

YOU DO:
1) Collect bits of yarn or string, dry cereal, macaroni, paper, sticks, pebbles, seashells.
2) Glue your odds and ends onto the paper, the inside of the box lid or food tray. (The lid and tray are ready-made frames for your work.)
3) Try using Popsicle sticks and buttons to create pictures and greeting cards. Sticks can make arms, legs and stems; buttons are good for faces, flowers and wheels.

Making Scrapbooks

YOU NEED:
sheets of paper (all the same size)
glue
ribbon, string or shoelace
scissors
magazines, newspapers, comics, labels from cans

YOU DO:
1) Cut out magazine or newspaper *pictures* and glue them on the sheets of paper. (Suggestions: babies, toys, cars, pets, houses, flowers, clothing.)
2) Cut out *words* you know and match them up with the pictures.
3) Save cards, gum wrappers or souvenirs from birthdays, trips or restaurants and add them to your scrapbook.
4) You can group similar pictures together on a page, like animals, things with wheels, favorite foods, etc.
5) Make a special cover, if you wish.
6) Punch 2 holes in each page and tie them all together with a ribbon, string or shoelace.
7) Now "read" your book by naming the pictures you have pasted.

Pressed-Leaf Designs

Take an autumn walk and gather some pretty leaves. Then ask Mother to help you press them into a picture. (If you can't iron them right away, press the leaves between the pages of magazines, weighted down by a heavy book.)

YOU NEED: fall leaves of different colors and shapes
crayons (optional)
waxed paper
newspapers
cardboard, construction paper or food tray
yarn or string
tape
warm iron
ironing board

YOU DO:
1) Arrange 2 or 3 leaves on the *bottom half* of the waxed paper. (Sprinkle bits of crayon around them if you wish.)
2) Now gently fold the *top half* of the waxed paper over your design.
3) Place a folded sheet of newspaper above and below the waxed paper and gently iron over it several times. (If an ironing board is not handy, a pile of newspapers will do.)
4) Make a frame by cutting a window (slightly smaller than your leaf picture) in the center of a cardboard food tray or piece of construction paper.
5) Tape the picture onto the back of the tray or paper frame.
6) Punch 2 holes at the top and tie on some yarn or ribbon.
7) Now hang up your picture in the window and let the sunlight shine through!

Rock Creatures

YOU NEED: rocks, all sizes and shapes
white glue
paint or cloth scraps

YOU DO:
1) Collect rocks on a walk around the block or on the beach.
2) Pick up *all kinds* — big and tiny, rough and smooth, round, pointed, flat, dark and light, speckled and white.
3) Glue the rocks together to make a variety of people and animals — a duck, an elephant, or whatever the shapes suggest to you.
4) For more colorful rock creatures, paint them or glue on cloth scraps for ears, tail, etc.

My Treasure Box

YOU NEED:

box with lid (egg cartons are especially good)
scissors, glue, crayons or paint
magazine pictures or construction paper
odds and ends like bottle caps, buttons, macaroni, straws, crepe paper, etc.

YOU DO:

1) Paint, color or cover your box with construction paper or magazine pictures. Decorate it with odds and ends and write your name on it if you wish.
2) Keep your favorite treasures in it, such as jewelry, baseball cards, keys, stones or stamps.

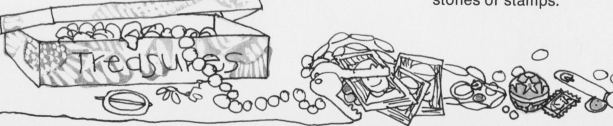

LET'S HAVE A RHYTHM BAND

It's easy and fun to make your own musical instruments. When you have finished, gather your friends and form a marching band. Turn on your radio or record player for background music.

Bells

YOU NEED:
spoon, stick or pencil
stem from a coffeepot

YOU DO:
While holding the stem, strike the bottom with the pencil, spoon or stick, or just strike 2 spoons together.

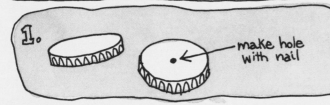

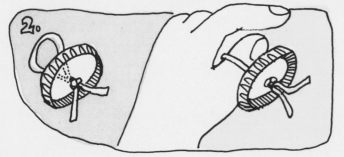

Finger Cymbals

YOU NEED:
2 small jar lids of the same size (baby food lids are just right)
piece of elastic, 4 inches long
hammer and nail

YOU DO:
1) Have Mother punch a hole in the center of each lid with the hammer and nail.
2) Push both ends of a piece of elastic through the hole, leaving a small loop the size of your finger on the top side of the lid. Keep your finger in the loop while Mother ties the ends into a large knot on the underside of the lid.
3) When you have made your 2 cymbals, put 1 on your middle finger, the other on your thumb; then clang them both together!

Comb Kazoo

YOU NEED:
comb
piece of waxed or tissue paper

YOU DO:
1) Fold the paper in half and wrap the teeth of the comb in the fold.
2) Put your lips over the fold and hum a tune moving the comb from side to side.

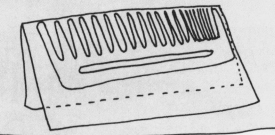

Drum

YOU NEED:
empty coffee can with a plastic lid or oatmeal box
masking tape
spoon, pencil with an eraser or stick
paper and crayons
yarn or string

YOU DO:
1) Secure the lid of your box or can with tape
2) Cover with paper and decorate with crayons.
3) Tie or tape on some yarn or string and hang the drum around your neck.
4) Use the stick, pencil or spoon for a drumstick.

Humming Flute

YOU NEED:
cardboard tube from paper towel or toilet paper roll
small piece of waxed paper
rubber band
pencil

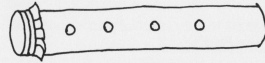

YOU DO:
1) With a pencil punch 3 or 4 holes (about 1 inch apart) in the side of a cardboard tube.
2) Cover one end with a piece of waxed paper held in place with a rubber band.
3) Hum a tune in the other end, moving your fingers over the holes.

Tambourine and Maraca

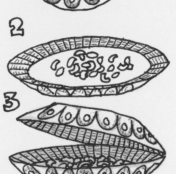

YOU NEED: 2 paper plates or foil pie pans (for tambourine)

small juice can or cardboard tube, foil, and rubber band (for maraca)

crayons, paint, ribbon or yarn, crepe paper and construction paper

dried beans, macaroni or pebbles

masking tape

glue

YOU DO:

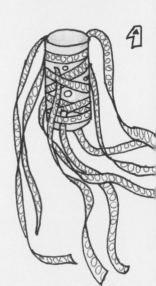

Tambourine

1) Decorate the plates or pie pans.

2) Put a handful of dried beans or macaroni on one plate.

3) Lay the other plate face *down* over the first plate and tape all around the edges (or punch holes and "sew" the sides together with yarn or ribbon).

4) Add crepe paper ruffles or streamers.

Maraca

1) Cover one end of the tube with foil or construction paper secured with tape or the rubber band.

2) Fill the tube with the beans, macaroni or pebbles.

3) Cover the other end as in Step 1.

4) Wind crepe or construction paper around the tube and decorate with streamers.

Now shake the instruments to the beat of the music!

Plink–a–Plink

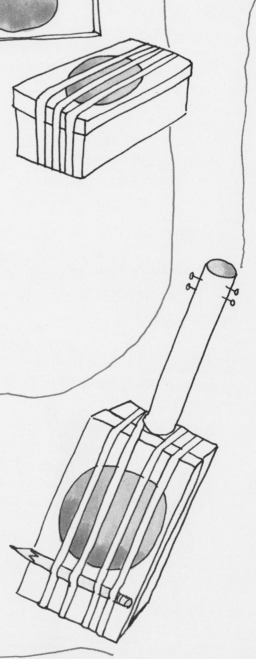

YOU NEED: sturdy shoe box with lid
rubber bands of different sizes, large
enough to fit around box
scissors

YOU DO: 1) Cut a large hole in the middle of the lid
before putting it on the box.
2) Stretch the rubber bands across the
opening of the box (about 1 inch
apart).
3) Now pluck your instrument over the hole
and notice the different sounds.

Do the tighter rubber bands sound different from the looser
ones? Do the thicker rubber bands sound like the thinner
ones? Which make the highest tones?

Banjo

1) Repeat directions for Plink-a-Plink.
2) Add a bridge by sliding half a cork, a pencil, or an eraser
under the rubber bands just above the hole.
3) For a handle, a long cardboard tube can be inserted into a
hole cut at one end of the box.

LET'S HAVE A MARCHING BAND

This song can be sung to the tune of "Yankee Doodle Dandy" or chanted without any tune. Join together in making the sounds of the instruments and move your hands as if you were playing them. You can use your homemade rhythm instruments, too.

We can play the big bass *drum*
　　This is the music to it
Boom, Boom, Boom goes the big bass drum
　　And this is the way to do it.

We can play the *tambourine*
　　This is the music to it
Ching, Ching, Ching goes the tambourine
　　And this is the way to do it.

We can play on the soldier's *horn*
　　This is the music to it
Toot, Toot, Toot goes the soldier's horn
　　And this is the way to do it.

Try adding some other instruments:

　　The old *banjo* goes plink, plink, plink
　　The *violin* goes zing, zing, zing
　　The silver *flute* goes toodle, toodle, doo

50

RHYTHM ACTIVITIES

Everybody Do This – Just Like Me

Two or more can play, taking turns being the leader.
There is only one verse, which is repeated over and over in a singsong way.

Everybody *do* this, *do* this, *do* this
Everybody *do* this . . . just like me!

Each time the verse is chanted, the leader makes a *different motion* and all join in with the same body movement. You might clap your hands, tap your feet, nod your head . . . and add more of your own.

Early in the Morning

(Tune of "Here We Go Round the Mulberry Bush")
Begin by singing the following verse, choosing actions that fit the words:

This is the way we wash our clothes,
Wash our clothes, wash our clothes,
This is the way we wash our clothes   (pretend to
So early *Monday* morning.   scrub clothes)

Other verses can be:
"This is the way we iron our clothes" or *"scrub our floor"* or *"sweep our house,"* etc., naming the days of the week in order.

Tap and Clap Your Favorite Song

YOU NEED: 2 or more children

YOU DO:
1) Gather on the floor and choose an easy song, like "Jingle Bells."
2) Now tap on the floor with the palm of your hands while you sing, keeping the beat.

   (tap) (tap) (tap) (tap) (tap) (tap)
   JIN — GLE BELLS JIN — GLE BELLS
3) Sing the song again, but this time, instead of tapping, *clap your hands* in time with the rhythm.
4) Now try tapping or clapping out the beat *without singing* at all.

Try another song. What about "Twinkle, Twinkle, Little Star"?

Choo-Choo Train

Choose a phrase like "Here Comes the Choo-Choo Train" and chant it over and over in different voices:

a whisper
LOUDLY
s-l-o-w-l-y
As fast as you can!

Who Stole the Cookie?

Take turns chanting these words with expression, using the names of the children playing.

Suzie asks: "Who stole the cookie from the cookie jar?"
Bill answers: "Ann stole the cookie from the cookie jar."
Ann says: "Who, me?"
Bill answers: "Yes, you."
Ann says: "Not me!"
Bill asks: "Then who?"
Ann says: "John stole the cookie from the cookie jar."
John answers: "Who, me?" etc.

Repeat until everyone has had a turn.

Ring Around the Rocket Ship

Ring around the rocket ship
    Try to grab a star
Stardust, stardust,
    Fall where you are.

All join hands in a circle and slide to the right. At the word "grab," drop hands and reach up. At the word "fall," fall to the floor. Repeat verse sliding to the left.

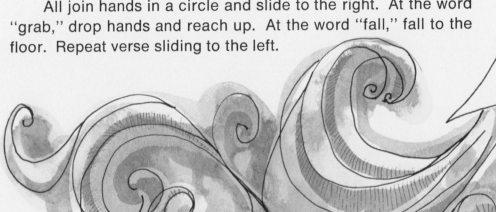

Who's Sitting on the Button?

YOU NEED: 4 or more players
small object such as button or penny

YOU DO:
1) One player is It and leaves the room.
2) The other players are seated, with one sitting on the button.
3) The person who is It returns and tries to guess who is sitting on the button by listening for the singing clues: the closer he comes to the hidden button, the louder the children sing; the farther away he moves, the softer they sing.
4) When the button is found, the player who was sitting on it leaves the room next.

FINGER GAMES

One Little, Two Little, Three Little Spacemen

One little, two little, three little spacemen . . .
Four little, five little, six little spacemen . . .
Seven little, eight little, nine little spacemen . . .
Ten little men in space!

Let each finger be a spaceman; start with your thumb and wiggle each finger in turn as you name the number.
Your fingers can also be: "Ten little jolly Santas," "Dancing dollies" or "Halloween pumpkins," etc.

Ten Little Martians

Ten little Martians
   Standing in a row   (hold up 10 fingers)

When they see the Captain   (bend fingers down and up)
   They bow just so

They march to the left   (move both hands with a
   And they march to the right   marching rhythm to the left,
                       then to the right)

Then they close their eyes   (palms together and under the
   And sleep all night.   side of the face, as if one
                       is sleeping)

Repeat the verse, using "nine little," "eight little," etc.

Two Little Dickie Birds

Two little Dickie Birds   (put fists together with two index
    sitting on a hill   fingers pointing up)

One named Jack   (wiggle the first finger of the right hand)

The other named Jill.   (wiggle the first finger of the left hand)

Fly away, Jack   (point the right finger over the right shoulder)

Fly away, Jill   (point the left finger over the left shoulder)

Come back, Jack   (bring back the right finger)

Come back, Jill   (bring back the left finger)

Open Shut Them

Open shut them   (open and close both hands)
Open shut them
Give a great big clap   (clap your hands)
Open shut them
Open shut them   (fold hands in lap)
Put them in your lap.

Window Watching

DAYTIME

What do you see when you look out the window?

Is it sunny today . . . or are there raindrops on the window?

What color is the sky? Do you see some fluffy clouds? Any birds or squirrels?

Can you tell the season by the way the trees look?

What kind of trucks do you see? Are there letters written on the sides?

Count the people you see walking. Are they dressed for a warm or a cold day?

Draw a picture of what you see.

NIGHTTIME

It's fun to look out the window just before bedtime.

What color is the sky at night?

Can you find the moon? What shape is it?

Where do you see lights? Look for moving or blinking lights.

Draw the night with chalk on dark paper.

A Rainy Day Walk in the House

Let's take a walk from room to room and look for special things.

Search for objects made of wood. Touch them all.
Can you find anything made of glass? Or metal? Or things that move? How many did you find of each?
Hunt for big things, hunt for blue things.
Hunt for pairs, opposites, and even things that grow.

A HOUSE HUNT CAN BE A GAME!

Two or more can play. Choose objects for your hunt, set a time limit, and see who can find the most.

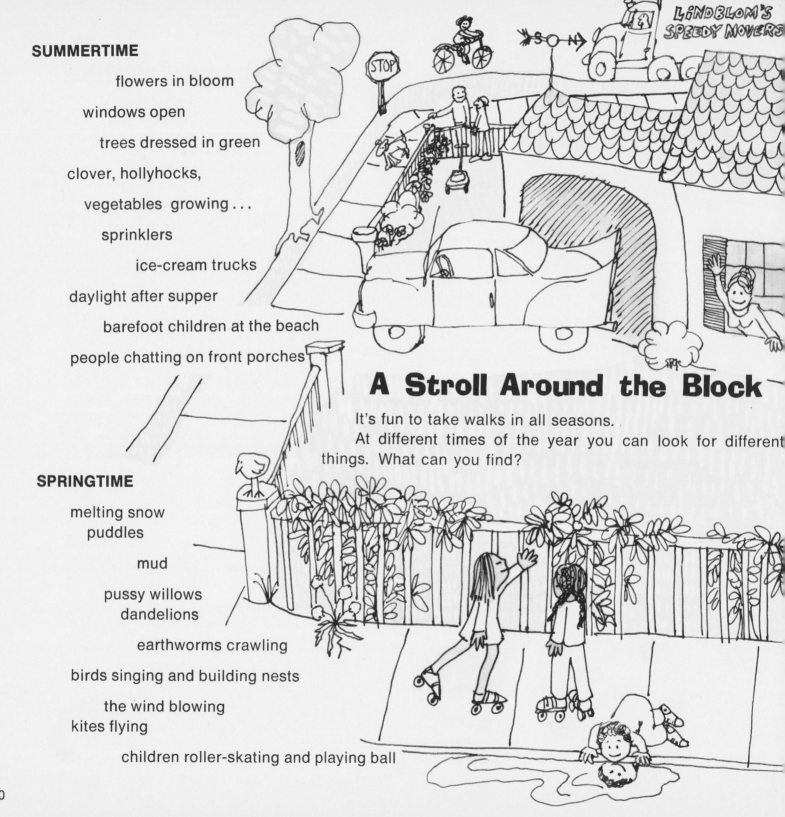

SUMMERTIME

flowers in bloom

windows open

trees dressed in green

clover, hollyhocks,

vegetables growing...

sprinklers

ice-cream trucks

daylight after supper

barefoot children at the beach

people chatting on front porches

A Stroll Around the Block

It's fun to take walks in all seasons.
At different times of the year you can look for different
things. What can you find?

SPRINGTIME

melting snow
puddles

mud

pussy willows
dandelions

earthworms crawling

birds singing and building nests

the wind blowing
kites flying

children roller-skating and playing ball

LINDBLOM'S SPEEDY MOVERS

60

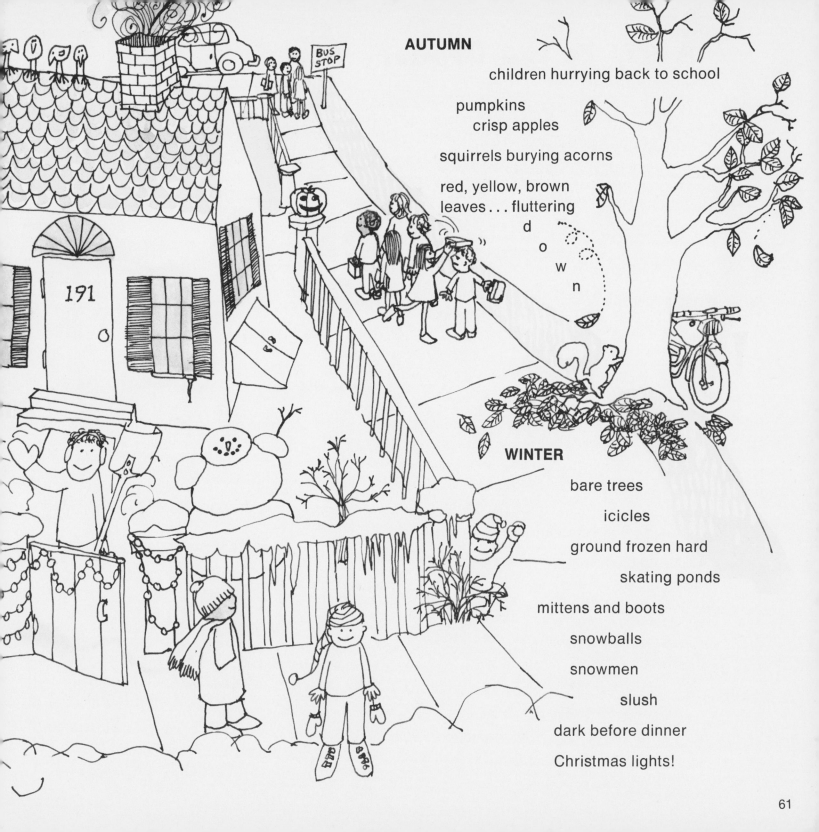

AUTUMN

children hurrying back to school

pumpkins
crisp apples

squirrels burying acorns

red, yellow, brown
leaves . . . fluttering
d
o
w
n

WINTER

bare trees

icicles

ground frozen hard

skating ponds

mittens and boots

snowballs

snowmen

slush

dark before dinner

Christmas lights!

61

A Trip to the Grocery Store

Go with Mother on her next trip for groceries. What do you see? Visit the fresh fruit and vegetable section. How many different colors can you find?

red	apples, beets, strawberries
yellow	lemons, pears, squash
orange	oranges, tangerines, carrots
green	limes, lettuce, spinach
white	onions, cauliflower
purple	grapes, cabbage

What sizes and shapes are the fruits and vegetables?

What is little and round?	an orange, a lime
What is big and round?	a grapefruit, a cabbage
What is long and thin?	a carrot, a celery stalk
What has an unusual shape?	a banana, a string bean, a pea pod
Which feel hard when you touch them?	potatoes, onions
Which feel soft?	grapes, berries
What is hard outside but soft inside?	a watermelon, a cucumber

Have you noticed that some fruits and vegetables are *fresh*? Some are *frozen*? And some are in *cans*?

Fun with Sounds

1) Close your eyes and *listen.*
   What sounds do you hear?
   Cars? Horns? Voices? An airplane?
   Which noises are loud?
   Which sounds are soft? Water running?

2) Put your fingers on your throat while you are singing a song.
   Can you feel something tingling on your fingers?

3) Speak into an empty oatmeal box and touch the bottom
   lightly with your fingertips.
   Can you feel the humming?

4) To play a *game with sounds,* have someone blindfold you
   and drop unbreakable objects on the kitchen floor (spoon,
   ball, plastic cup).
   Listen carefully and try to identify what you hear.
   For a variation, have Mother hide an object in a covered box
   and shake it.
   Now can you guess what it is by its sound?
   Night is the best time for listening. Be very quiet . . . can
   you hear a clock ticking?
   Shhhh

Fun with Shapes

1) Find some circles
   in your house.
   Do you see a clock?
   A cookie? A plate?
   A penny?

2) Make some circles on a
   piece of paper by drawing
   around a glass, a can or a
   jar lid. Color them with your
   crayons

3) Now cut out the circles and
   count them. Which is the
   biggest? The smallest?

**THIS IS A CIRCLE
IT IS ROUND**

**THIS IS A TRIANGLE
IT HAS 3 SIDES**

Fold your square napkin in
half (from corner to corner)
What do you have now?

This looks like
a piece of
pie or a
witch's hat!

1) Point to the corners and count them.

2) Look for some things in the kitchen that are square: a box, a napkin, a slice of bread.

HERE IS A SQUARE
IT HAS 4 SIDES

3) Measure the 4 sides. Are they the same?

4) Draw a square on the sidewalk with a rock or chalk. Then hop from corner to corner.

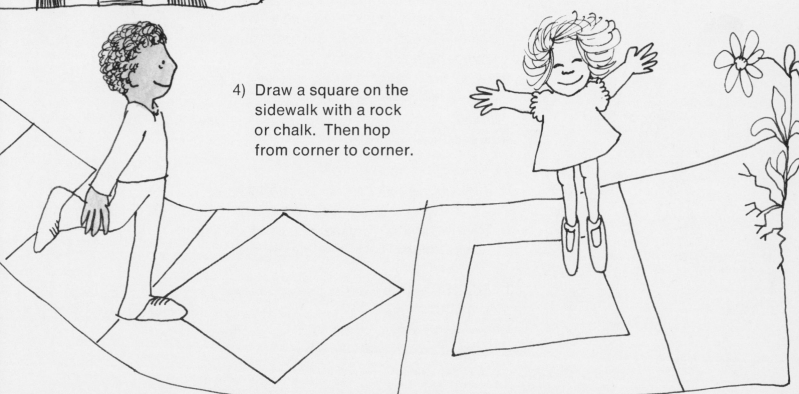

Taste It, Sniff It, Feel It

YOU NEED: small amounts of foods to *taste:* pieces of cheese, bread, apple, banana; grains of salt, pepper, sugar, cinnamon; dabs of mustard, mayonnaise, peanut butter

items to *sniff* (with distinctive odors): onion, catsup, coffee, vinegar, vanilla, cocoa, spices

items to *feel:* small stones, sponge, clay, cotton, bottle caps, hair rollers, emery board

handkerchief or scarf

tray (optional)

YOU DO:
1) First put all the objects on the table or tray and let everybody see them.
2) Then 1 person closes his eyes or is blindfolded with a handkerchief or scarf.
3) The others give him the items to identify, one at a time.
4) Everyone takes turns tasting, sniffing, touching . . . and guessing.

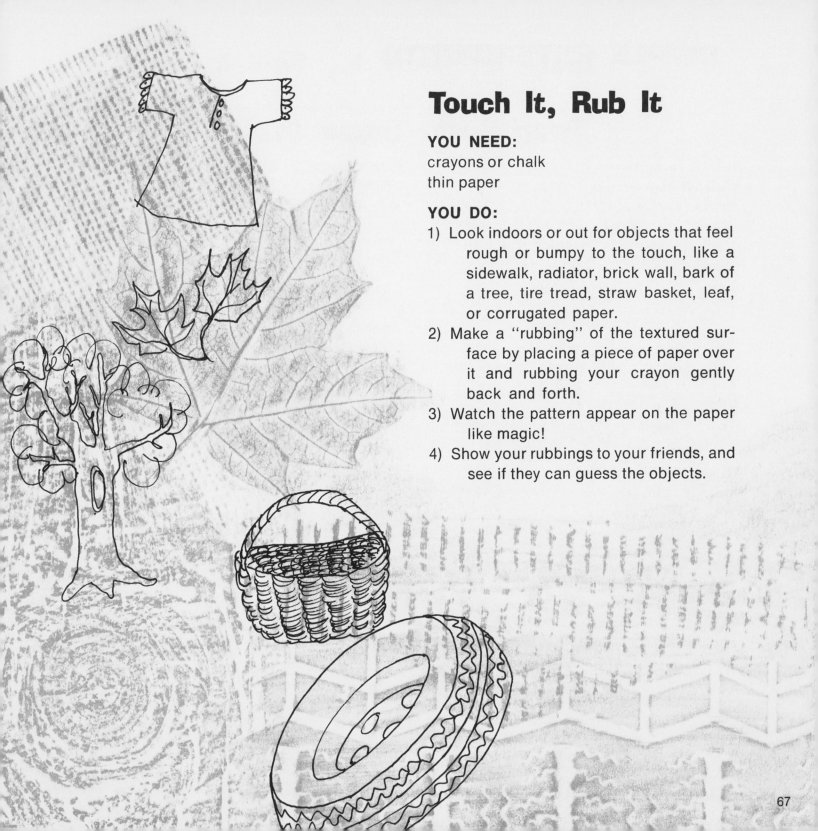

Touch It, Rub It

YOU NEED:
crayons or chalk
thin paper

YOU DO:
1) Look indoors or out for objects that feel rough or bumpy to the touch, like a sidewalk, radiator, brick wall, bark of a tree, tire tread, straw basket, leaf, or corrugated paper.
2) Make a "rubbing" of the textured surface by placing a piece of paper over it and rubbing your crayon gently back and forth.
3) Watch the pattern appear on the paper like magic!
4) Show your rubbings to your friends, and see if they can guess the objects.

SIMPLE EXPERIMENTS

Soap Push – Sugar Pull

YOU NEED:

bowl or cup of water
pepper *or* broken bits of a toothpick, matchstick, cork, or wood shavings
piece of soap
sugar

YOU DO:

1) Sprinkle pepper or other lightweight material over the water and see it float.
2) Now dip a small piece of soap into the water. What happens to the pepper? (It should float away from the soap.)
3) Next, sprinkle sugar into the water. What happens now? (The floating bits should run toward the sugar.)

The pepper moves away because of an oily film given off by the soap. Sugar acts like a sponge and draws the water toward it.

Cup Full of Air

YOU NEED:

bowl of water
glass
paper towel or piece of newspaper

YOU DO:

1) Crumple the towel or newspaper and stuff it inside the glass.
2) Turn the glass upside down and quickly plunge it into the bowl of water, touching the bottom.
3) Quickly lift the glass straight out of the water, being careful not to tip it.
4) Take the paper out of the glass. Is it wet or dry? (Why should it be dry?)
5) Repeat Steps 1 and 2. Then lift the glass out of the water, tipping it to one side. What happens this time? Why?

Fizzle Fun

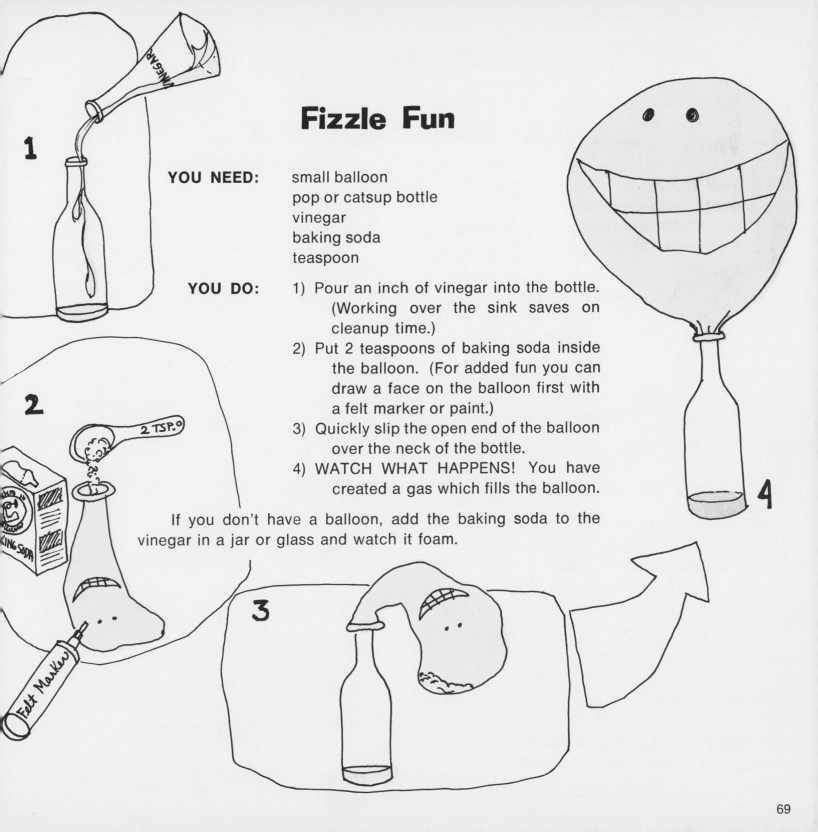

YOU NEED:
small balloon
pop or catsup bottle
vinegar
baking soda
teaspoon

YOU DO:

1) Pour an inch of vinegar into the bottle. (Working over the sink saves on cleanup time.)
2) Put 2 teaspoons of baking soda inside the balloon. (For added fun you can draw a face on the balloon first with a felt marker or paint.)
3) Quickly slip the open end of the balloon over the neck of the bottle.
4) WATCH WHAT HAPPENS! You have created a gas which fills the balloon.

If you don't have a balloon, add the baking soda to the vinegar in a jar or glass and watch it foam.

Traveling Heat

YOU NEED:
bowl of hot water
wooden spoon or pencil
metal spoon or fork

YOU DO:
1) Have Mom fill the bowl with hot water.
2) Dip the pencil or wooden spoon into the water and hold it there a few seconds. Does it feel warm?
3) Now try holding the metal spoon in the water. Does it feel warm? Why? Try some other objects and see what happens.

Heat travels through metal but not through wood.

Icy Wonder

YOU NEED:
ice cubes
dry glass jar with lid

YOU DO:
1) Fill the jar with ice cubes and cover tightly with the lid.
2) Leave the jar on the kitchen counter for at least 15 minutes and see what happens: to the ice, to the outside of jar.

Magic Hands

YOU NEED: 3 bowls filled with hot (careful, not too hot), warm and cold water

YOU DO:
1) Line up the containers in this order: hot, warm, cold.
2) Put one hand in the hot water and one in the cold at the same time.
3) Now quickly put *both* hands into the warm water.

Presto! The cold hand feels hot and the hot hand feels cold. Surprise your friends with this trick.

MAKE A KITCHEN GARDEN

Sweet Potato Plant

YOU NEED:
sweet potato with buds
glass jar
toothpicks

YOU DO:
1) Put the sweet potato into a glass jar with the small end of the potato down. Use toothpicks to hold it up if the mouth of the jar is too large.
2) Add water. Always have enough to wet the bottom of the potato.
3) Keep in a sunny place and watch the roots grow down and the green leaves grow up.

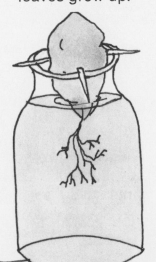

Growing Carrot Tops

YOU NEED:
carrot tops
small stones
saucer

YOU DO:
1) Cut off the tops of some carrots and put them in a saucer. Surround them with several small stones to hold them in place.
2) Always keep a little water in the dish.
3) Wait a week and see what happens.

Fruit Seeds

YOU NEED:
seeds from oranges, lemons, apples, grapefruit or pumpkins
egg carton, jar or paper cup
soil

YOU DO:
1) Let the seeds dry for 2 or 3 hours.
2) Fill an egg carton, jar or paper cup with soil. Plant the seeds near the top.
3) Water each day. Watch them grow.

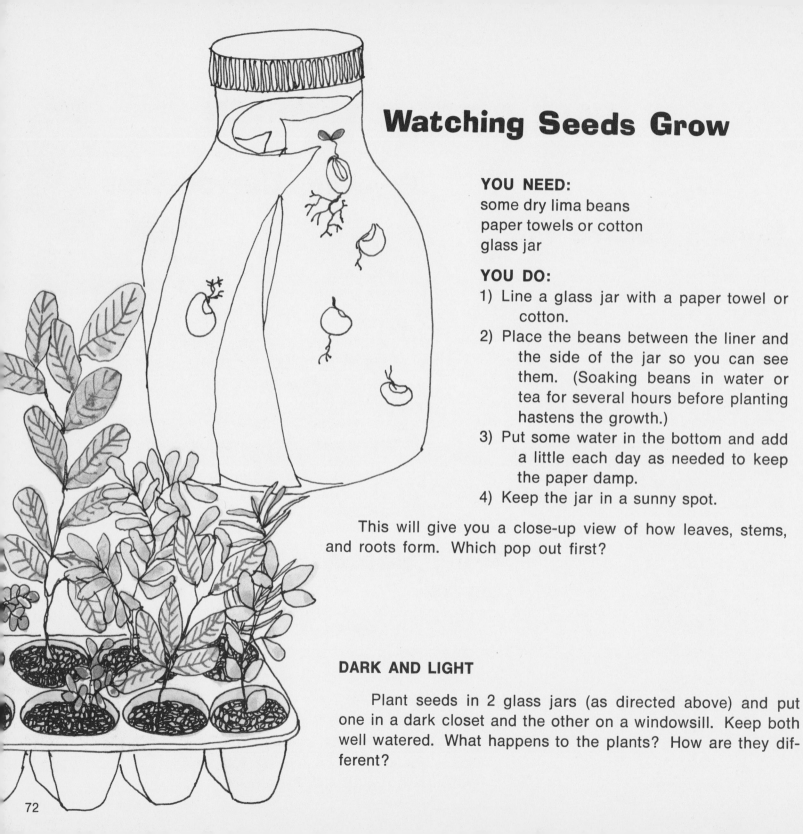

Watching Seeds Grow

YOU NEED:
some dry lima beans
paper towels or cotton
glass jar

YOU DO:
1) Line a glass jar with a paper towel or cotton.
2) Place the beans between the liner and the side of the jar so you can see them. (Soaking beans in water or tea for several hours before planting hastens the growth.)
3) Put some water in the bottom and add a little each day as needed to keep the paper damp.
4) Keep the jar in a sunny spot.

This will give you a close-up view of how leaves, stems, and roots form. Which pop out first?

DARK AND LIGHT

Plant seeds in 2 glass jars (as directed above) and put one in a dark closet and the other on a windowsill. Keep both well watered. What happens to the plants? How are they different?

Guess What I'm Doing

A pantomime game

YOU NEED:
2 or more players

YOU DO:
1) Each player takes turns acting out something he likes to do, *without talking.*
2) One player might pretend that he is sweeping. He moves his arms back and forth as if he were holding a broom.

3) The others try to guess what he is doing. The player who guesses "sweeping" takes his turn next.
4) He might "swim" or "pitch a baseball," "wash dishes," "hammer a nail" or "rock a baby."
5) He could also imitate an animal: "hop like a bunny," "swing like a monkey," etc.

What will *you* do? (If a younger child needs help, whisper an idea in his ear.)

What's in Mother's Purse?

YOU NEED: whatever happens to be in Mother's purse: comb, compact, keys, pencil, glasses case, coins, hankie, tissue, etc.

YOU DO:

1) First shut your eyes, or use a handkerchief as a blindfold.
2) Mother takes objects out of her purse, one at a time. Feel each one and try to guess what it is *without* looking.
3) To make the guessing a bit harder, Mother can wrap the objects in a handkerchief or hide them in her coin purse.

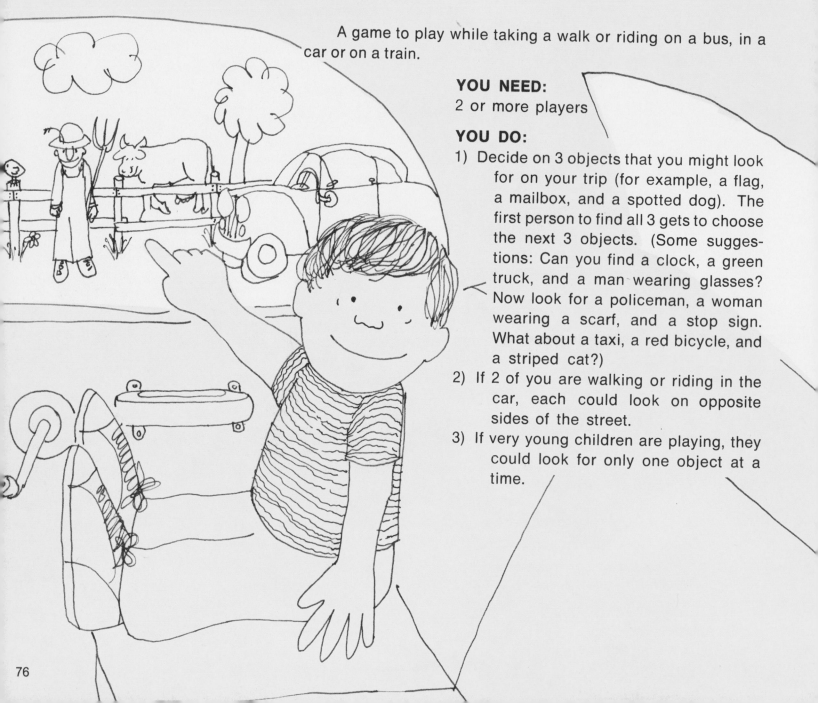

Looking as We Go

A game to play while taking a walk or riding on a bus, in a car or on a train.

YOU NEED:
2 or more players

YOU DO:

1) Decide on 3 objects that you might look for on your trip (for example, a flag, a mailbox, and a spotted dog). The first person to find all 3 gets to choose the next 3 objects. (Some suggestions: Can you find a clock, a green truck, and a man wearing glasses? Now look for a policeman, a woman wearing a scarf, and a stop sign. What about a taxi, a red bicycle, and a striped cat?)

2) If 2 of you are walking or riding in the car, each could look on opposite sides of the street.

3) If very young children are playing, they could look for only one object at a time.

Matching Pairs

YOU NEED: pairs of everyday objects, such as spools, spoons, pencils, keys, buttons, bottle caps, crayons, combs, socks, etc.
box or bag

YOU DO:
1) Ask Mother to put pairs of objects into a bag. Have her start with just a few and add more as you progress.
2) Dump the contents onto the floor and pair them up.

Those over four might use "related" objects, such as: comb and brush, soap and washcloth, shoe and sock, envelope and stamp, snapshot and negative.

Name the Object

A matching game for 2 children.

YOU NEED: 2 paper bags
pairs of everyday objects (as in Matching Pairs)

YOU DO:
1) Each player is given a paper bag containing the same objects.
2) The first player takes an object (spoon) from his bag and says, "Give me your *spoon*."
3) The second player reaches in his bag *without looking* and finds the matching spoon. He says, "Here is my *spoon*."
4) Take turns until all pairs are found.

Calendar Toss

YOU NEED:
page from large calendar *or* crayons and cardboard to make your own
button, bottle cap or coin for marker (different one for each player)

YOU DO:

1) Place the calendar on the floor and use it as a target.
2) Each player takes turns tossing his marker onto the calendar.
3) Younger children could try to hit a circled date (birthday, holiday, etc.).
4) Older children might aim for high numbers to see who can score the most points, or they might try to hit the numbers in order, one at a time (as in hopscotch), or score either on odd or even numbers.

Rock Teacher

YOU NEED:
stairs or sidewalk
any small object that will fit in your hand (thimble, rock, penny)

YOU DO:

1) All of the players (pupils) sit on the floor in front of the bottom step (the kindergarten). Or, if you play on the sidewalk, let each square represent a different grade, and number it with chalk.
2) One person is "teacher" and hides the object in one of his hands. Each "pupil" in turn guesses which hand is holding the penny or rock.
3) If he points to the correct hand, he moves to the first step (first grade). If he guesses the wrong hand, he must stay where he is.
4) Each time the "pupil" guesses correctly, he moves up another step, to "second grade," "third grade," etc. The first person to move all the way up to the top is the winner and becomes the new "teacher."

Keep a Secret

A good party or rainy day game.

YOU NEED:

3 or more players
spool, thimble, bottle cap, penny or paper
  clip

YOU DO:

1) One person is It. All the others leave
   the room. The one who is It hides
   the spool or other small object some-
   where in the room where it can be
   seen without *moving* anything. (Under a chair, on the windowsill, behind
   a lamp, or beside a table leg.)
2) The other players come back into the
   room to hunt for the spool. When
   someone sees it, he walks away, sits
   down, and says nothing, trying to
   keep the hiding place a secret!
3) After *everyone* is sitting down, the *first
   player* to find it now picks up the
   spool, and becomes It for the next
   game.

Call the Colors

YOU NEED:

sheets of construction paper (a different
  color for each player)
scissors
paper bag

YOU DO:

1) From each piece of construction paper,
   cut a 2-inch strip, divide it into 4 small
   squares and put them into the paper
   bag.
2) Each player chooses one of the *large*
   colored squares and stands on it.
3) One player who is the "caller" pulls a
   square out of the bag and names its
   color, for example, "red."
4) The player standing on red says, "I'm
   on red," and gets to keep the small
   colored square.
5) The first player to get all 4 of his matching squares wins and becomes the
   next caller.
6) For the next round, everyone moves to
   another color and the small squares
   are shuffled and put back into the bag.

String Hunt

YOU NEED: string or straws
scissors

YOU DO:

1) Cut the string or straws into many pieces of varying lengths.
2) One player hides the strings (on the windowsill, behind a curtain, beside the chair leg, in an ashtray, etc.) while the others are out of the room.
3) The players are called back into the room for the hunt.
4) When all of the strings have been found, each player places his own, *end to end*, on the floor in front of him. The winner is the player whose strings form the *longest line*, not the one who has the most strings.

If you have a yardstick, it's fun to measure the lines.

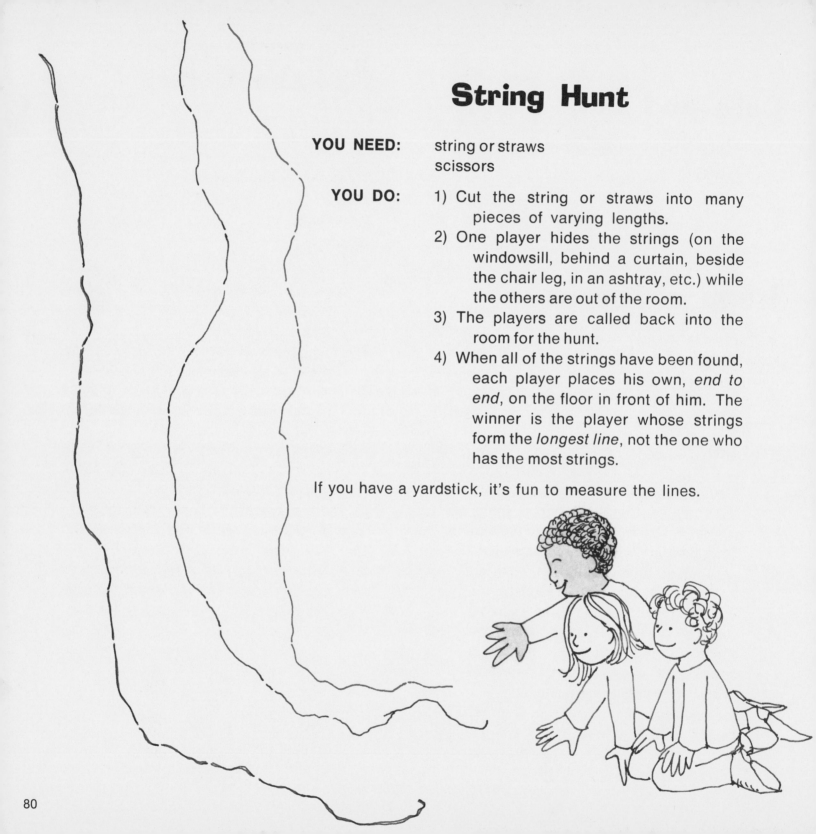

Cats and Dogs

This makes a particularly good party game.

YOU NEED: wrapped candy, peanuts or pennies
2 small paper bags or juice cans (one marked "Cats," the other "Dogs")

YOU DO:

1) Hide the candy, or nuts or pennies around the room or yard before the guests arrive.
2) Divide everybody into 2 teams: the Cats and the Dogs. Have the Dogs practice saying "Woof woof" and the Cats "Meow meow."
3) Choose a captain for each team and give him his "team bag."
4) At the "go" signal, everyone hunts for the hidden objects. When a player finds one, instead of picking it up, he must meow if he is a Cat or bark if he is a Dog, until his captain comes to put the candy into the "team bag." Then he continues to hunt for more.
5) When all the goodies have been found, count them; the team with the most wins. The captains then divide the winnings among their teammates.

...meow

...WOOF WOOF....

WORD GAMES

I Saw a Purple Cow

YOU NEED: 2 or more players

YOU DO: 1) The first player says, "I saw a purple cow on the road. I *one* him."
2) The next player says, "I *two* him."

3) Whoever is next says, "I *three* him," and each in turn says:
"I *four* him"
"I *five* him"
"I *six* him"
"I *seven* him."
4) Then whoever's turn is next says, "I *eight* him." He gets a big laugh, because it sounds like "I *ate* him!"

This game can be played over and over, each time changing the object. All kinds of things can be named: "I saw a wiggly worm," an old tin can, a funny little man, a red-eyed witch — the sillier, the better!

I 8 Him!

Aunt (sitting) AND uncle (standing)

Opposites

YOU NEED: a parent and 1 or more players

YOU DO:
1) Mother thinks of a word; then you give its opposite. For example, Mother says, "In"; you say, "Out." Mother says, "Up"; you say, "Down."
2) Now *you* try to think of a word and let Mom name its opposite.

Look around the room for ideas: the door may remind you of "open and close." The light switch might suggest "on and off" or "dark and light"; the water faucet — "wet and dry"; a chair — "sit and stand." Looking at people helps you to think of opposites, too: "sister–brother," "aunt–uncle," "boy–girl," "tall–short," "fat–thin."

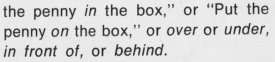

Penny in the Box

YOU NEED:
small box with lid
tiny objects, such as pennies, small stones or bottle caps

YOU DO:
1) Let Mom begin the game by giving the first direction. She might say: "Put the penny *in* the box," or "Put the penny *on* the box," or *over* or *under*, *in front of*, or *behind*.
2) Take turns with Mom giving the directions. You might say: "Put two or three pennies *under* the box," or whichever words you choose.

Try playing this game at cleanup time, by putting your shoes *in* the closet, the book *on* the shelf, etc.

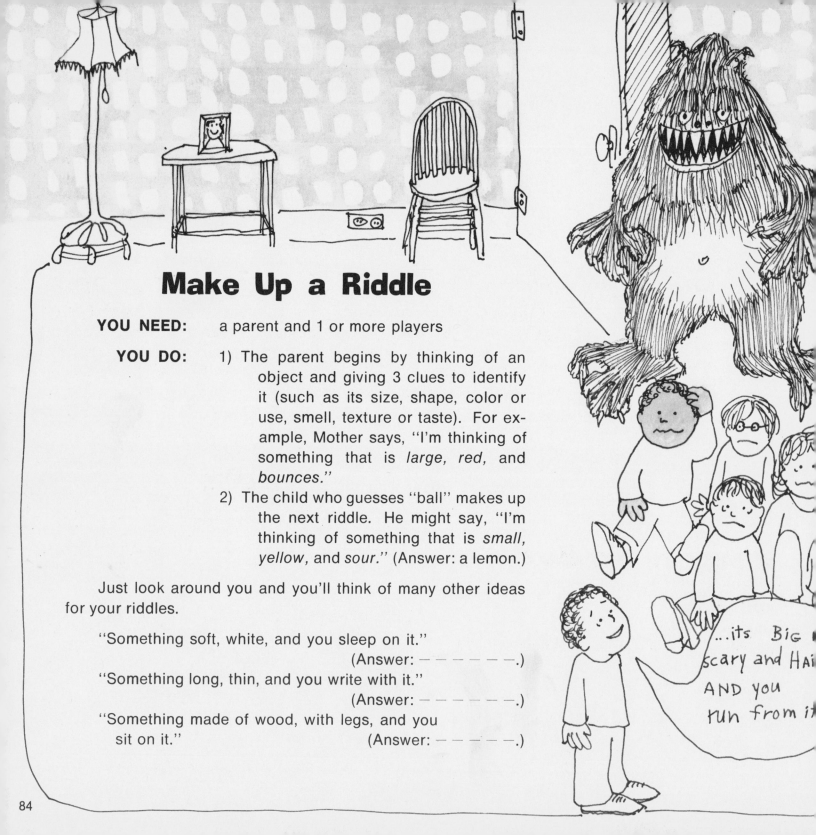

Make Up a Riddle

YOU NEED: a parent and 1 or more players

YOU DO: 1) The parent begins by thinking of an object and giving 3 clues to identify it (such as its size, shape, color or use, smell, texture or taste). For example, Mother says, "I'm thinking of something that is *large, red,* and *bounces.*"

    2) The child who guesses "ball" makes up the next riddle. He might say, "I'm thinking of something that is *small, yellow,* and *sour.*" (Answer: a lemon.)

Just look around you and you'll think of many other ideas for your riddles.

"Something soft, white, and you sleep on it."

        (Answer: — — — — — —.)

"Something long, thin, and you write with it."

        (Answer: — — — — — —.)

"Something made of wood, with legs, and you sit on it."   (Answer: — — — — —.)

...its BIG scary and HAI AND you run from it

I See Something Red

YOU NEED:
2 or more players

YOU DO:
1) One person begins the game by looking around him and spying an object
   . . . a book, a tie, a shirt, a pencil . . .
   and *names the color.*
   He says, "I see something red."
2) The others take turns guessing what it
   is. "Is it an apple?" "Is it that boy's
   red shirt?" "Is it that red book on the
   table?"
3) The answer is "no" until someone
   guesses right. This person then
   chooses the next object and says, "I
   see something green . . . or yellow . . .
   or blue," or whatever color the object is.

Find Me Another

YOU NEED:

1 or 2 children, with a parent or older child

5 items that are the same: pennies, bottle caps, spoons, etc.

YOU DO:

1) Mother begins the game by hiding 5 pennies in the room, separately, in places that are easy to find.

2) You come into the room to hunt for the pennies.

3) As you find each penny, bring it to Mother, who says, "I have *one* penny, find me another." You respond, "You have one penny, I'll find another."

4) When you bring the second penny, Mother says, "I have *two* pennies, find me another." You answer in the same way before looking for the third penny.

5) After all the pennies are found, count them aloud.

PARTY THEMES

A party for from five to seven children, lasting one to two hours, seems to work out best, especially for the very young.

Half the fun of the party is making your own invitations, favors and refreshments. First choose a theme; then all of your planning can center on that one idea.

1) Circus

2) Trains and Planes

3) Mother Goose

4) Comic Strip Charact (Peanuts, Li'l Abner, et

5) Outer Space

6) "Dress-up" Tea Party

7) Holidays (Halloween, Valentine's Day, Fourth of July, Easter)

8) Bring Your Favorite D

9) Cowboys, Indians, Pirates

10) Sports: Baseball, Football, Hockey

11) Fairy Tales: Cinderella, Snow White

12) Springtime: Bird Butterflies, Flowers

Invitations

YOU NEED: paper or cardboard
envelopes
scissors
glue
crayons or felt pens

YOU DO:
1) Cut a piece of paper slightly smaller than your envelope.
2) Draw a picture that fits your theme or cut one out from a magazine or newspaper; paste it onto your invitation.
3) Be sure to include your name, the date, time, and place.
4) Instead of using a store-bought envelope, you can make your invitation twice the size, fold it in half and tape or staple it together (writing your message on the inside).

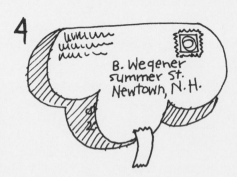

It's fun to deliver the invitations to your friends yourself, or if they live too far away, drop them into a mailbox. (Ask Mother for a stamp.)

Table Decorations

A *centerpiece* makes the party table look special. Find a toy to match the theme, or make one yourself.

CENTERPIECE IDEAS:

1) For a train theme use a toy or shoe box train
2) "Dress-up" — a "grown-up" hat, scarf, etc. on a doll or a balloon face

3) Circus or zoo — stuffed or paper animals in a cage made either from a box or two cardboard food trays with straws for bars
4) Space — a rocket ship made of cardboard tubes covered with foil
5) Holidays — pumpkin Pilgrim or a paper-plate Easter bonnet

A basket is a good container for a centerpiece. You can put wrapped favors in it with yarn or ribbon running to each person's place.

Styrofoam makes a useful base for a table decoration for any occasion. Just cover it with crepe paper of an appropriate color and insert straws or toothpicks to attach paper cutouts which fit the theme: flags for the Fourth of July, scarecrows for Halloween, hearts for Valentine's Day, etc.

Balloons always add a festive touch to any party.

Favors

There is no need to buy party favors. You can make them ahead of time or enjoy making them as a party activity with your guests.

TREASURE TUBE

Fill empty juice cans or cardboard tubes with candy, popcorn, peanuts, pennies, tiny toys, etc. Tape the tops and bottoms closed and then decorate them with crepe or tissue paper.

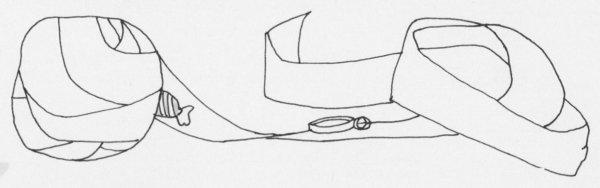

SURPRISE BALL

Wrap tiny prizes, one at a time, with crepe paper strips, forming a ball as you wind. For added interest, glue or paint on a face.

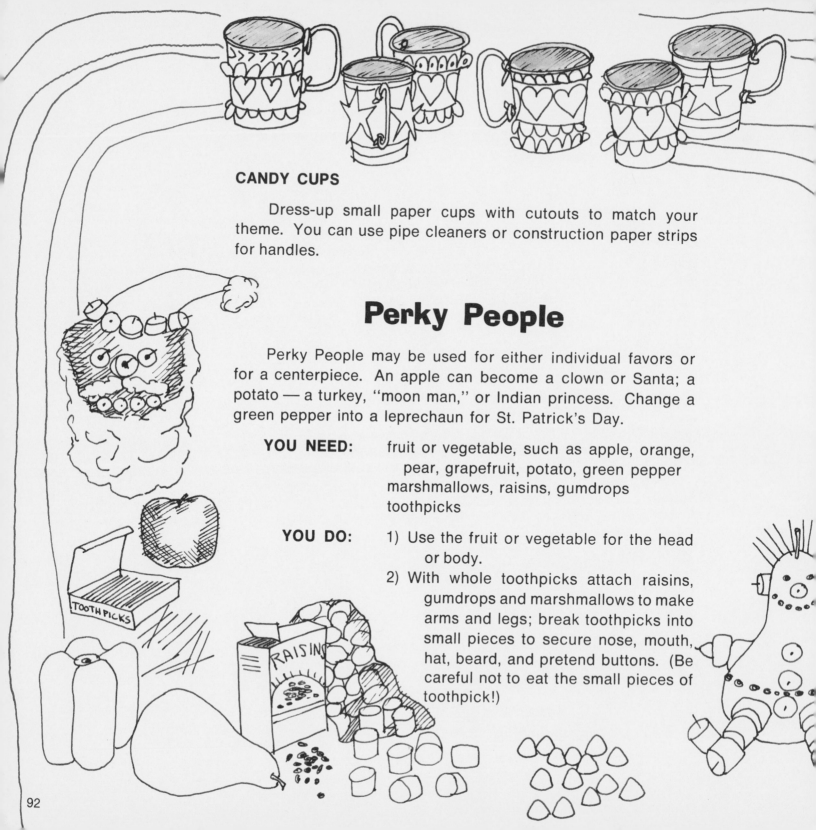

CANDY CUPS

Dress-up small paper cups with cutouts to match your theme. You can use pipe cleaners or construction paper strips for handles.

Perky People

Perky People may be used for either individual favors or for a centerpiece. An apple can become a clown or Santa; a potato — a turkey, "moon man," or Indian princess. Change a green pepper into a leprechaun for St. Patrick's Day.

YOU NEED: fruit or vegetable, such as apple, orange, pear, grapefruit, potato, green pepper
marshmallows, raisins, gumdrops
toothpicks

YOU DO:
1) Use the fruit or vegetable for the head or body.
2) With whole toothpicks attach raisins, gumdrops and marshmallows to make arms and legs; break toothpicks into small pieces to secure nose, mouth, hat, beard, and pretend buttons. (Be careful not to eat the small pieces of toothpick!)

TOOTH PICKS

RAISINS

Party Hats

YOU NEED:

paper plates, foil pie plates or cardboard food trays

materials for trimming: scraps of construction paper, tissue or crepe paper, foil, paper doilies, ribbon, yarn, feathers, etc.

glue or cellophane tape

a long ribbon or string

YOU DO:

1) Make a slit or hole on each side of the plate and run a string or ribbon through the holes for tying under your chin.

2) Glue or tape trimmings on your hat, such as crepe paper flowers and ruffles, cardboard-animal cutouts, free-form yarn designs.

OTHER IDEAS:

For a tassel, dangle an egg carton cup from a piece of yarn.

Attach cardboard stand-up figures by poking them through slits in the hat.

Decorate a round carton (like an oatmeal box) with polka dots for a clown hat.

Look through the book to find other ideas for gifts and favors, such as Bathtub Boats, Macaroni Jewelry, puppets, Fun Dough figures, and rhythm toys.

Party Foods

Refreshments are always the best part of any party. Choose foods that will be decorative as well as tasty, keeping the theme in mind.

DESSERTS AND SWEETS

Turn an ice-cream cone (with a scoop of ice cream in it) upside down for a clown.

Fill a tiny flowerpot or paper cup with ice cream and top it with a lollipop for a flower.

Create:

A clown or Santa from an apple and marshmallows

An Indian brave or a daisy with a cookie and apple slices

Marshmallow or gumdrop animals with toothpicks

Fancy cupcakes decorated with candy hearts, chocolate sprinkles, animal crackers, or candy corn

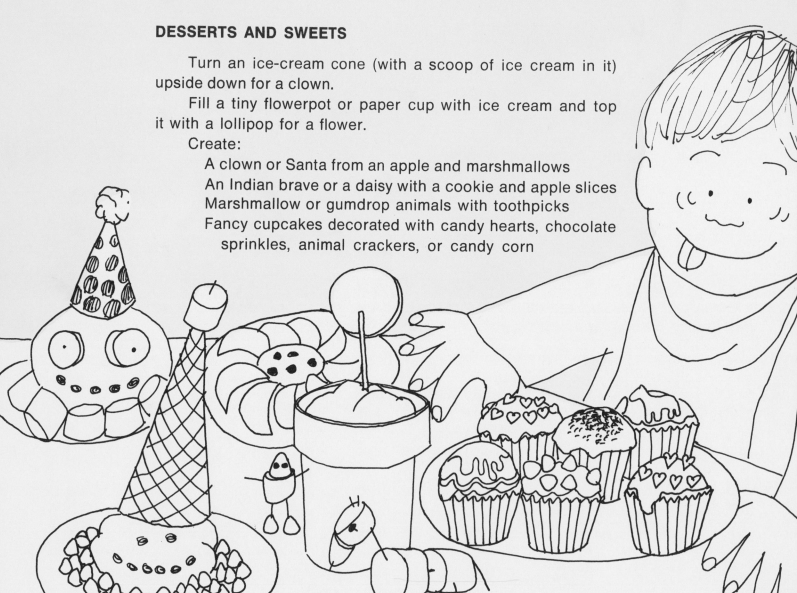

DRINKS

Serve a colorful fruit drink to match your holiday theme (like orangeade for Halloween). Add ginger ale to make a bubbly punch.

For a special touch:

Make ice cubes with fruitade (you can even put a strawberry or a cherry in the center of each cube).

Decorate straws with paper cutouts. Just push the straw through 2 slits in the cutout.

You can make festive napkin rings by having Mother slice a cardboard tube into 1-inch circles for you to decorate.

PARTY GAMES

Many of the games found in this book are perfect for parties. Most are adaptable for any number of players. Just change the objects used in the games to fit the party theme. For example: 1) Change "I Saw a Purple Cow" to "I Saw an Orange Pumpkin" or "a Mean Witch" for a Halloween party.

2) In "Rock Teacher" many objects can be used in place of a rock: hearts for Valentine parties, earrings for a "dress-up" party.

3) Adapt an old favorite, "Pin the Tail on the Donkey," to "Pin the Hat on the Witch," "the Arrow on the Valentine Heart," "the Beard on Santa Claus." (Magazine pictures make good targets. Masking tape, rolled into a circle, is recommended instead of pins.)

4) For the "String Hunt" use yarn, choosing a color to fit your party theme, like green or red for Christmas, or assorted ribbon from the birthday presents.

5) Play "Keep a Secret" but use a birthday card, Christmas ornament, paper turkey, or an Easter egg for the hidden object.

6) With "Calendar Toss" use the month and date of a holiday or birthday.

7) Substitute a holiday or birthday card for the button in "Who's Sitting on the Button." Sing or clap an appropriate song ("Jingle Bells," "Yankee Doodle," "Happy Birthday to You").

8) Instead of "Cats and Dogs," use goblins and witches, cowboys and Indians, Santas and bells, making their appropriate sounds. You could also hide peanuts for a circus or pet theme, candy hearts for Valentine's Day, etc.

Your older brothers and sisters will enjoy playing game numbers 4, 5, 6, and 7 with you — or at their own parties, too.